CORNERSTONES OF FREEDOM™

IMMIGRATION

BY PETER BENOIT

CHILDREN'S PRESS®

An Imprint of Scholastic Inc.
New York Toronto London Auckland Sydney
Mexico City New Delhi Hong Kong
Danbury, Connecticut

BRINGING
HISTORY
to LIFE

Content Consultant
James Marten, PhD
Professor and Chair, History Department
Marquette University
Milwaukee, Wisconsin

Library of Congress Cataloging-in-Publication Data
Benoit, Peter, 1955–
    Immigration/by Peter Benoit.
        p. cm.—(Cornerstones of freedom)
    Includes bibliographical references and index.
    ISBN-13: 978-0-531-23057-2 (lib. bdg.)   ISBN-10: 0-531-23057-0 (lib. bdg.)
    ISBN-13: 978-0-531-28157-4 (pbk.)   ISBN-10: 0-531-28157-4 (pbk.)
    1. United States—Emigration and immigration—History—Juvenile
literature. 2. United States—Emigration and immigration—Government
policy—Juvenile literature. 3. Immigrants—United
States—History—Juvenile literature. I. Title.
    JV6450.B45 2012
    304.8'73—dc23   2011031343

Printed in the United States of America 113
SCHOLASTIC, CHILDREN'S PRESS, CORNERSTONES OF FREEDOM™,
and associated logos are trademarks and/or registered trademarks of
Scholastic Inc.

1 2 3 4 5 6 7 8 9 10 R 21 20 19 18 17 16 15 14 13 12

Photographs © 2012: Alamy Images: 23 (Everett Collection), 37 (Lyroky), 57
bottom (Thomas Frey/imagebroker); AP Images: 47 (Alfred J. Hernandez/The
Sun), 48 (Denis Poroy), 51 (Harry Cabluck), 49 (Lynne Sladky), 41 (National
Archives), 11, 16, 19 (Northwind Picture Archives), 54, 59 (Steven Senne), 44;
Bridgeman Art Library/Peter Newark American Pictures: 32; Corbis Images/
Frederick C. Howe/National Geographic Society: 5 bottom, 31; Dreamstime/
Sumnersgraphicsinc: back cover; Getty Images: 29 (General Photographic
Agency), 18 top, 56 top (J. Singleton Copley/Hulton Archive), 4 top, 46, 50
(John Moore), 27 (Lewis W. Hine), 55 (Spencer Platt); Granger Collection: 4
bottom, 34 (Arnold Genthe), 28 (Lewis Hine), cover, 5 top, 12, 13, 17, 22, 24, 36;
Library of Congress : 20, 40 (Detroit Publishing Co.), 10 (Edward S. Curtis), 18
bottom (John Neagle), 42 (Lewis W. Hine), 30 (Underwood & Underwood), 8;
Superstock, Inc.: 38 (Everett Collection), 14 (Image Asset Management Ltd.),
2, 3, 39 (Spaces Images), 7 (Steve Vidler); The Image Works/Roger-Viollet:
43, 57 top; U.S. Navy Photo/Abbie Rowe: 6 (National Park Service/John F.
Kennedy Presidential Library and Museum).

Maps by XNR Productions, Inc.

Did you know that studying history can be fun?

BRING HISTORY TO LIFE by becoming a history investigator. Examine the evidence (primary and secondary source materials); cross-examine the people and witnesses. Take a look at what was happening at the time—but be careful! What happened years ago might suddenly become incredibly interesting and change the way you think!

Contents

4

A Nation of Immigrants

President John F. Kennedy's family originally came to the United States from Ireland.

U.S. president John F. Kennedy once called the United States "a nation of **immigrants**." People from around the world come to its shores in search of greater freedom and **economic** opportunities. Their energy and optimism has fueled the country's growth. They have created

PRESIDENT KENNEDY WAS THE

new businesses and provided labor for existing ones. Some immigrants have taken on important roles in the country's government.

Immigrants have also helped to bring together traditions from all over the world. Their languages, religions, and celebrations have all blended over time and created the unique American culture that we know today.

But the immigrant experience has also been filled with difficulties. Many people throughout history have feared immigrants. As a result, immigrants have often been treated poorly. Most have faced major struggles in their efforts to succeed in the United States. Poverty, disease, and hunger have been common among the nation's newest arrivals. But immigrants have thrived in the United States despite these hardships.

On St. Patrick's Day, Irish Americans celebrate the culture of their homeland.

GREAT-GRANDSON OF IRISH IMMIGRANTS.

CHAPTER I

THE FIRST IMMIGRANTS

Huge numbers of Irish immigrants came to America during the Irish potato famine.

AMERICA HAS BEEN A LAND OF immigrants since its earliest days. People have left their homelands and traveled to America for many reasons. Some have left to seek new opportunities when their homelands experienced social and economic problems. Others have fled from failed revolutions, unfair governments, and overcrowding. Disasters such as the Irish potato famine in the 1800s prompted large numbers of people to immigrate. Immigrants have sometimes been drawn to America by its open spaces and quality farmland. Others have been drawn by promise of religious and political freedom.

Native Americans settled in what would become the United States and Canada long before European settlers first arrived in the late 1400s.

Natives and Colonists

Immigration is a great risk. People must often leave everything behind when they move to a new country. But this risk can result in a real improvement in a person's quality of life. Immigrants are generally neither the richest nor the poorest people in their homelands. But they are often less well off than average. Many lack opportunities for advancement. They relocate for social, economic, and personal reasons. Some relocate to be with family and friends who have already immigrated. Even the earliest immigrants entered America seeking to improve their lives.

American immigration began tens of thousands of years ago. What is now Alaska was once connected to Asia by a land bridge. Humans arrived in America as they chased bison herds across the land bridge and into Alaska. They eventually worked their way south and east across what are now the United States and Canada. They developed new civilizations and became the people that we know as Native Americans. Their populations grew, and millions of people were living in America by the time the first European immigrants arrived.

Spanish settlers founded the colony of Saint Augustine in the mid-1500s in what is now Florida. French and British explorers soon followed Spain's lead. Great Britain's King James I had seen Spain grow fabulously wealthy when its explorers discovered gold in the Americas. He decided that Great

Saint Augustine, Florida, is the oldest permanent European settlement in what is now the United States.

Bartholomew Gosnold and his men were among the first British settlers in North America.

Britain should establish American colonies of its own. Overseas colonies would extend Britain's influence and reduce the pressures of an increasing population at home. Some British citizens quickly saw good reason to leave for America. British laws passed all of a man's lands to his firstborn son when he died. This left younger sons with fewer economic opportunities than their older brothers. They saw America as a place where they could have land of their own.

Lawyer and explorer Bartholomew Gosnold promoted American colonization among his friends and neighbors in London. On April 10, 1606, he received a royal charter, or permission, from King James I to establish a colony called Virginia.

The 104 men and boys of the Virginia Company set sail half a year later. They landed in 1607 and established a settlement called Jamestown. The colony struggled in its early years. The settlers faced disease, poor water quality, and a lack of food. They also experienced warfare with Native Americans from time to time. Jamestown did not fully succeed until colonist John Rolfe began growing tobacco several years later. Money from tobacco crops began flowing into the colony. Supply ships brought workers and farmers to help settle America's land.

Another British colony named Plymouth was established around this time. It was settled in part by a group of people who traveled to America on the *Mayflower* in 1620. The rate of British migration to America rose sharply in

The first women arrived in Jamestown over a year after the colony was founded.

Plymouth's founders sailed to America aboard the *Mayflower*.

the 1630s. Many of the settlers were workers, servants, and farmers who hoped for better lives in America. Most were very young. Some traveled as **indentured servants**. They rested their hopes in future freedom.

A FIRSTHAND LOOK AT
THE MAYFLOWER COMPACT

The Plymouth colonists drew up an agreement called the Mayflower Compact when they arrived in America. The compact was an agreement to create laws and a government for the common good. The original document has been lost, but its words live on. See page 60 for a link to read the text of the Mayflower Compact online.

Growth in the Colonies

More and more immigrants traveled to America as the colonies grew and new ones were formed. A man named George Calvert founded a colony named Avalon in 1621 in what is now Canada. Harsh winter weather prevented most of Avalon's colonists from succeeding. Many moved to Virginia in the hopes of growing tobacco. But many of the Avalon colonists were followers of the Catholic Church. Most of Virginia's colonists were Protestants, members of the Church of England. They looked on the Catholics with contempt. Calvert decided to start a new colony where Catholics would not have to deal with poor treatment by the Protestants.

Calvert returned to England and attempted to secure a royal charter for lands north of Virginia. He met with resistance in Protestant England and died before the charter was granted. But Calvert's son Cecilius succeeded in securing the charter. He set off for America to found the Maryland Colony. A Protestant uprising eventually swept the Calvert family from power in the colony. Their charter was taken away in 1692. It was only restored a few decades later when the Calverts converted to Protestantism.

John Rolfe recorded the arrival of the first enslaved Africans in Virginia in August 1619. Just under 3,000 more Africans were captured and shipped to America by 1660. Their numbers in America swelled to 300,000 in the next 100 years.

Immigration increased sharply in the 1700s. People from many countries began moving to America. They spoke a variety of languages and often came from very different cultures. Germans, French Huguenots, and Protestant Scotch-Irish immigrants settled in South Carolina. Welsh and Germans settled in Pennsylvania. Finns and Swedes were common in Delaware. The Dutch founded New York. This meant that each of America's colonies had its own distinctive culture. Several languages were often spoken in a single settlement. One missionary was surprised to find that 18 different languages were spoken in New Amsterdam (today's New York City) when he visited in 1643.

Roughly 250,000 Europeans were living in America by 1700. Hundreds of thousands more immigrated

Enslaved Africans played a major role in the development of the American colonies.

New Amsterdam was home to immigrants from all around the world.

to the colonies between 1700 and 1776. German
Mennonites and French Huguenots fled religious
discrimination in their home countries. Irish farmers
came to America because land was plentiful. Eighteenth-
century immigrants were often poor farmers. Others
learned the skills to make useful goods. The French
immigrant Apollos Rivoire apprenticed as a silversmith.
He passed along his knowledge to his son, Paul Revere.
Revere went on to become an important figure in the

Paul Revere

Paul Revere was born on January 1, 1735. He apprenticed as a silversmith under his French immigrant father, Apollos Rivoire. Revere was exposed to the ideas of men who were against British authority in the colonies. He became a member of the Sons of Liberty. The Sons of Liberty was a group of colonists who fought against British oppression. Revere and the Sons of Liberty played a central role in the famous Boston Tea Party. He is perhaps best known for alerting the colonial troops of British soldiers' movements before the Battles of Lexington and Concord in the American Revolution. This helped the colonists win the very first battle of the war.

American Revolution. Other immigrants used their talents to help shape America's landmarks. Pierre-Charles L'Enfant helped develop the street plan of Washington, D.C.

Blacksmiths molded raw metal into useful tools.

British immigration to America slowed considerably by 1800. The British government passed the Passenger Vessels Act of 1803. It was intended to prevent immigrants from being **exploited** by shipping companies. This meant that the shipping companies had to provide better service to immigrants. It also meant a rise in the cost of immigrating to America. Many people could no longer afford the journey. Fewer immigrants who were not slaves entered the United States in the first decade of the 1800s. But America stood open to a great wave of immigration that would transform it forever.

TODAY'S PERSPECTIVE

Parliament's Passenger Vessels Act of 1803 was meant to ensure a safe voyage for British citizens. But it also increased the expense of traveling to America. This increased cost acted as a barrier to many who wanted to leave. This slowed the loss of population in Great Britain. Historians now understand that the law was also meant to address the loss of skilled workers who fueled the country's Industrial Revolution. More workers allowed British companies to develop new technologies. It also helped the country maintain its powerful position in the Industrial Revolution against nations that had more natural resources.

CHAPTER 2

POPULATION EXPLOSION

Many immigrants settled in New York City.

THE 1800S AND EARLY 1900S were marked by explosive population growth in the United States. Immigrants led the way in this growth. The total U.S. population, excluding slaves, was approximately 9.6 million in 1820. It was almost 10 times as high by 1910. The immigrant population grew at a faster rate than the population as a whole.

These immigrants moved to the nation's largest cities in much greater numbers than earlier Americans had. Only 1 in 14 Americans lived in a city in 1820. But by 1910, about half of the country's population lived in cities.

Many families starved during the Irish potato famine.

The Irish in America

Until 1860, most U.S. immigrants came from Great Britain, Ireland, and Germany. During the first half of the 1800s, one-third of all immigrants came from Ireland. That number increased when the Great Famine struck in 1845. Ireland's population had grown rapidly in the previous 50 years. But Ireland had barely been touched by the Industrial Revolution. Its economy depended on agriculture. The large population increase meant that there was not enough land for everyone to farm.

Poor Irish farmers began to rely mainly on potatoes for food. Potatoes did not require as much space to grow as most other crops. They were also easier to grow. But a fungus struck the country's potato crop in 1845. The problem stretched on for several years. Many Irish starved. More than one million Irish died from diseases. Around the same number left for America.

Poor Irish turned their thoughts to a new life in the United States. Ships regularly left Irish ports for Canada. This meant that many of the immigrants traveled to Canada before journeying to the United States. Some made the trip from Canada to the United States on foot. Many Irish immigrants settled in Boston, Massachusetts. The city's population of 137,000 was 25 percent Irish by 1850. Irish immigrants also settled elsewhere in the country.

YESTERDAY'S HEADLINES

Anti-Irish feelings were common throughout the United States. People openly spoke out against Irish immigrants. They often refused to hire Irish people for jobs. The September 4, 1830, issue of the *New York Evening Post* contained an advertisement looking for a cook. It read, "Wanted. A cook or chambermaid. . .must be American, Scotch, Swiss or African—no Irish."

This type of attitude was accepted by much of society at the time. Irish immigrants were forced to take the most dangerous and the lowest-paying jobs in the country.

Anti-Irish feelings began to spread as more and more Irish immigrants came to the United States. Most Irish people were Catholic. But the majority of the U.S. population was Protestant. The problem grew worse by mid-century as the Irish immigrants flocked to the United States during the famine.

Large numbers of Irish immigrants found jobs as laborers and servants. The Irish were often hired for especially dangerous work. Even slaves were not forced to do some of the jobs that the Irish did. Slaves sold for as much as $1,500 at auction. They were considered too valuable to risk. Thousands of Irish laborers worked to dig New York's Erie Canal. Thousands more were hired to dig the New Basin Canal in New Orleans, Louisiana.

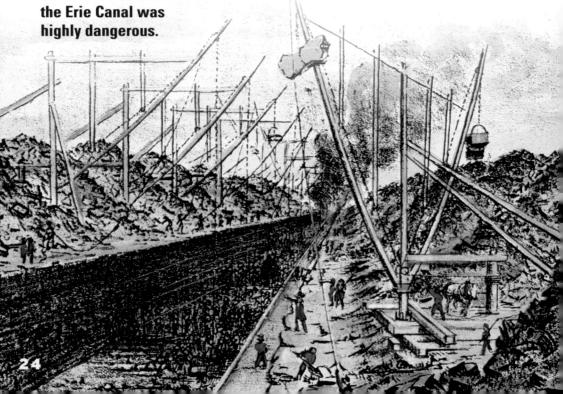

The construction of the Erie Canal was highly dangerous.

As many as 20,000 of these Irish workers may have died from disease or accidents.

Some Irishmen sought fortunes in California during the gold rush. One of them was James Phelan. Phelan sold supplies to miners and became one of San Francisco's first millionaires.

A Clash Over Catholicism

The influence of the Catholic Church grew as Irish and German immigration increased. Many Americans began to associate all immigrants with Catholicism. Irish

A VIEW FROM ABR★AD

No one looked on the Irish experience in America with greater interest than people back in Ireland. Many Irish songwriters wrote songs about the experiences of Irish immigrants in America. Ballads such as "The Green Fields of America" spoke of the promise of life in a new land. Others such as "Paddy's Lamentation" recounted the key role Irish soldiers played in the Union army during the Civil War. Many songs dealt with the dangers Irish immigrants faced in their new home. These songs often featured characters who missed their beautiful homelands as they struggled to make lives for themselves in America.

Catholics also became influential in **urban** politics. Most of them became members of the Democratic Party. Some, such as William Tweed of New York, became influential political bosses. These bosses ensured that immigrants would vote for Democratic candidates by creating jobs. Many Protestant citizens were upset by the growth of Catholicism. They were suspicious of the Irish political leaders. These leaders often engaged in unfair practices to get their way. Tweed's organization held large-scale ceremonies to **naturalize** immigrants before elections. This increased the number of voters who would support the party during the elections.

Many Protestants began to see Irish immigration as a threat. Some even burned down Catholic churches in protest. Insurance companies stopped insuring Catholic churches and businesses. Anti-Catholic groups appeared around the country calling for a change in immigration policies. They eventually united into a political party called the Know-Nothing Party in the 1850s. Party members staged a variety of protests. They rigged elections in Baltimore, Maryland, to make sure their candidates won. They tarred and feathered a Catholic priest in Maine. Others started an Election Day riot in Louisville, Kentucky. But they were unable to change immigration law.

A FIRSTHAND LOOK AT
THOMAS NAST'S POLITICAL CARTOONS

Thomas Nast, a German immigrant, was a cartoonist for *Harper's Weekly*. His cartoons often dealt with the mistrust of political leaders such as William Tweed. See page 60 for a link to view one of Nast's political cartoons online.

German immigrants (shown here) were often treated with more respect than Irish immigrants were.

German immigrants did not attract the same degree of suspicion that the Irish did. They did not cluster in urban centers. The German population was instead spread between farms and cities. This made them seem less threatening to many Americans. They were generally less politically active than the Irish as well.

German immigrants were also less likely to be poor. Many left Germany because industrialization threatened their jobs. They chose to become immigrants instead of changing jobs. Many were skilled tradesmen. They worked as machinists, tailors, and bakers. German farmers often lived in communities populated mainly by other Germans. German language and culture thrived in these communities. But not all German immigrants lived in such communities. Some learned to speak English and began to adopt American culture.

Urban Germans lived in **ethnic enclaves** such as Over-the-Rhine in Cincinnati, Ohio. Over-the-Rhine became famous for its detailed brick buildings and a choral music festival called Sängerfeste. Kleindeutschland (Little Germany) on the Lower East Side of Manhattan was another well-known German enclave. St. Louis, Missouri, and Milwaukee, Wisconsin, were also home to large German populations.

Most German immigrants were Protestant. This meant they did not face the same type of discrimination the Irish

German immigrants shared meals at dining halls in ethnic enclaves.

Germany and the United States fought each other during World War I.

did. But they faced resistance when they fought to have German adopted as the main language in schools where they formed a majority. Some schools compromised by offering instruction in both English and German. But many state and local governments outlawed this practice in the 1920s. The laws came partly in response to anti-German feelings that arose because Germany and the United States were on opposite sides during World War I. Still, the influence of German culture was widespread. German operas, symphonies, and plays were performed throughout the country.

Swedish immigrants left their home country from port cities such as Gothenburg.

Scandinavian Immigrants

Scandinavian immigrants made up a smaller part of the American population than the Germans or the Irish did. Swedish farmers were hungry for better land and more of it. They also hoped for a greater degree of religious freedom than was allowed by Sweden's Lutheran Church. Many of them migrated to **rural** areas in the upper midwestern states. Others established an ethnic enclave called Swede Town in Chicago, Illinois. Swedish immigrants ran stores, saloons, and bookshops in Swede Town. Swedish language books and newspapers were sold there.

At the same time, the rising population in Norway encouraged farm families to migrate to rural America. These Norwegian immigrants established themselves in close-knit communities. More than half relocated to Minnesota, Wisconsin, and North Dakota. Quality farmland was plentiful in those states. Norwegians also established a significant ethnic enclave in Brooklyn, New York. Like the Swedes, Norwegians founded newspapers, schools, and colleges in the last half of the 1800s.

The Danes were by far the smallest of the Scandinavian immigrant groups. Many chose not to form separate ethnic enclaves. They instead lived and worked with Americans. As a result, they were more quickly absorbed into the American culture.

Norwegian immigrants sometimes wore the traditional clothing of their homeland.

CHAPTER 3

DIVERSITY

California became a popular destination for Chinese immigrants during the gold rush of 1849.

CHINESE IMMIGRANTS BEGAN arriving in California in large numbers during the early months of the 1849 gold rush. They established their own mining camp after being excluded from other camps. Chinese Camp soon grew to include 5,000 miners. Many Americans grew frustrated as Chinese immigration increased. Chinese miners often were able to extract gold after American miners had abandoned claims. Chinese laborers also worked for less than their native-born counterparts. Chinese immigration surpassed 20,000 in 1852. By this time, the goldfields were already becoming less productive. American gold miners blamed Chinese workers for low wages and for the economic decline following the Civil War. Chinese workers were frequently beaten or imprisoned.

Many Chinese immigrants made their homes in the growing city of San Francisco.

Other Ethnicities

The California **legislature** passed a foreign miners tax in 1852. It was aimed specifically at the Chinese. But the Chinese miners persisted in working despite the financial burden it created. An act designed to restrict Chinese immigrants was passed on February 19, 1862. The act made it illegal for Americans to bring Chinese immigrants to the United States. It was the first U.S. law ever to restrict immigration. A more comprehensive law called the Chinese Exclusion Act was put in place in 1882 to suspend Chinese immigration. But immigration of other groups continued unrestricted.

Beginning in the 1890s, larger numbers of immigrants came from the Mediterranean, eastern Europe, and East Asia. Italians alone accounted for four million immigrants between 1880 and 1920. Most Italian immigrants flocked to large cities. Others settled in California, where they grew grapes and made wine. Large numbers of them went to New England and the mid-Atlantic states. Italian immigrants settled throughout New York City. They paved streets and built railroads. Some worked in stores. They made their way as both unskilled and semiskilled workers.

Anti-immigrant attitudes continued to spread throughout the country. Two Italian immigrants, Ferdinando Sacco and Bartolomeo Vanzetti, were accused of murder in Braintree, Massachusetts, in 1920. Many

A VIEW FROM ABROAD

People all around the world paid close attention to the trial of Sacco and Vanzetti. Many believed that the two Italian immigrants were being treated unfairly because of anti-immigrant feelings in the United States. Protesters burned American flags in South Africa. Protest strikes closed factories across South America. British writer H. G. Wells spoke out against the treatment of Sacco and Vanzetti in the October 16, 1927, issue of the *New York Times*. He believed that the courts were not focusing on the murder itself. They were instead focusing on the ethnicity and political background of the two men.

historians believe that ethnic discrimination prevented the men from receiving a fair trial. They were executed in 1927.

The diversity of America's population expanded further in the late 1800s and early 1900s. Greeks, Armenians, and Arabs began immigrating in large numbers. Greeks were widely distributed throughout the country. A large majority of them eventually settled in cities. They helped build railroads, worked in meatpacking and mining, and opened restaurants.

Arabs formed large populations in Detroit and New York. Many worked as traveling vendors. These jobs required them to interact with the general public. They worked especially hard to learn the English language and American customs because of this. Most Arabs were followers of Islam. They eventually began to construct

The Sacco and Vanzetti case made headlines across the country.

The first mosque in the United States was built in Cedar Rapids, Iowa, in 1934.

religious buildings called mosques. Mosques became sources of tension in smaller communities. Some Arabs responded by abandoning Islam and converting to Christianity. Others simply moved.

Large numbers of Armenian immigrants settled near Fresno, California. They faced broad discrimination. They became the target of laws barring them from settling in wealthier Fresno neighborhoods. Such laws were used elsewhere against Jews and Italians to limit their opportunities. In 1948, the United States Supreme Court finally ruled these laws illegal in *Shelley v. Kraemer*.

A FIRSTHAND LOOK AT
ELLIS ISLAND

Ellis Island served for more than 60 years as the nation's busiest port of entry for immigrants. It saw the arrivals of more than 17 million new Americans. Video footage captured the arrival of immigrants in 1903, as they embarked on a new life. See page 60 for a link to view the footage online.

Regulation

In 1892, the U.S. government opened an immigrant reception center on Ellis Island in New York Harbor. Ellis Island processed more than 17 million immigrants between 1892 and its closing in 1954. As immigrants sailed into the harbor, one of the first sights they saw of America was the Statue of Liberty. The statue was a

Thousands of immigrants arrived at Ellis Island each day.

The Statue of Liberty became an important symbol of American freedom for immigrants arriving at Ellis Island.

symbol of freedom given to the United States by France in 1886. Emma Lazarus's poem "The New Colossus" was inscribed on a bronze plaque inside the Statue of Liberty. The poem promised that America would welcome the "huddled masses yearning to breathe free." But the statue was made at a time when restrictive laws began to close the country's "golden door."

The Contract Labor Law of 1885 made it illegal for businesses to import most foreign workers. Immigrants had fueled the Industrial Revolution in America. But some lawmakers argued that foreign workers led to lower wages and decreased the quality of life for all workers. In 1891, Congress approved a law excluding immigrants suffering from contagious diseases from

Many Jewish immigrants formed communities in New York City.

entering the country. People who had been convicted of crimes were also excluded.

Jews from eastern Europe began immigrating in large numbers around the end of the 1800s. Previous Jewish immigrants had mainly come from Germany. They had already established themselves well in America. They often looked down on the poor, rural newcomers from eastern Europe. As a result, the two groups often settled in separate ethnic neighborhoods. They had few contacts outside their groups. Most new arrivals from eastern Europe entered at Ellis Island. They lived in tiny apartments in New York's Lower East Side. Many had jobs in the clothing industry. They worked in unsafe shops where fires started easily.

In 1911, a fire broke out in a scrap bin on the eighth floor of the Triangle Shirtwaist Company factory. The flames spread quickly through the 10-story building. Dozens of workers jumped or fell to the concrete sidewalk 100 feet (30 meters) below. Most were young women. The doors leading to the exits were all locked. One hundred and forty-six people died.

Poles, Jews, and Hungarians settled mainly in northeastern cities. Most had been rural peasants in their homelands. They now built railroads and helped to industrialize America. Most Polish immigrants were loyal to the Catholic Church. They maintained a strong sense of ethnic identity because of organizations like the Polish National Alliance.

Roughly 450,000 Hungarians came to America in the 15 years preceding World War I. Most were young men. They worked dangerous jobs such as coal mining and

SPOTLIGHT ON

Triangle Shirtwaist Factory Fire

The 1911 fire at the Triangle Shirtwaist Company factory was the worst industrial disaster in New York City history. In just 18 minutes, the flames killed 129 women and 17 men. Almost all of them were immigrants from Europe. They tried to escape by the building's fire escape and down fire truck ladders. But the fire escape fell apart under the weight of so many people, and the fire trucks did not have tall enough ladders.

The fire led to major changes in the nation's labor laws. More than 30 new laws were passed as a result of the fire. Some required business owners to make their buildings safer. Others prevented children from working long hours.

construction. More than 20,000 **refugees** fled Hungary after World War II ended in 1945. Hungary had been occupied by the Soviet Union after losing the war. Many Hungarians were unhappy with the major changes the Soviets made to their government. Another 35,000 Hungarians moved to the United States after a revolution against the government failed in 1956. Many settled in New York City and Cleveland, Ohio.

Japan's industrial development had forced many of the country's farmers to leave. They immigrated to America and established family farms in California. A few became wealthy businessmen and owned thousands of acres of land. Their success fueled anti-Japanese feelings.

Some Hungarian immigrants worked on farms in the Midwest.

California lawmakers considered laws similar to the 1882 Chinese Exclusion Act to block Japanese immigration.

But President Theodore Roosevelt did not want to anger the Japanese government with such laws. The United States and Japan signed the Gentlemen's Agreement in 1907. The agreement stated that the Japanese government would not allow

President Theodore Roosevelt agreed not to restrict Japanese immigration.

laborers to move to the United States. The United States agreed to pass no laws against Japanese immigration. The agreement permitted Japanese immigration to reunite families. This agreement remained in effect for less than 20 years. The Johnson-Reed Act of 1924 made major changes to U.S. immigration laws. It placed strict limits on how many immigrants of each nationality could enter the country. It did not allow any Asian immigrants at all.

CHAPTER 4

ON THE BORDER

Many Europeans found refuge in the United States when their home countries were occupied by enemy soldiers during World War II.

THE 1952 IMMIGRATION

and Nationality Act established **quotas** for immigration. It also determined that refugees displaced by wars or disasters would be counted separately from other immigrants. The 1952 law did away with the racial restrictions of the Johnson-Reed Act, but regional and national quotas continued until 1965. The act also addressed American fears of **communism**. It allowed **deportation** of immigrants with Communist Party connections. It blocked their entry into the country as well. The law did not restrict families that were immigrating to reunite. And it allowed workers with important skills to bypass the quota system. The law reflected the nation's struggle to find the proper balance for a complex issue.

Many illegal Mexican immigrants travel dangerous paths through the desert in order to enter the United States.

Illegal Immigration

Illegal immigration caused Congress to consider further changes in the 1980s. The 1986 Immigration Reform and Control Act made it necessary for employers to confirm that their workers were not illegal immigrants. Four years later, the Immigration Act of 1990 brought more changes to U.S. immigration laws. It placed limits on the number of immigrants allowed into the country to reunite with families. It also limited the number of immigrants allowed in because of their job skills.

The 1990 act also established a controversial lottery program encouraging countries with low levels of emigration to send more of their people to the United

States. In addition, the law attempted to crack down on illegal immigration from Mexico by strengthening the U.S. Border Patrol.

Border Security Today

On September 11, 2001, organized terrorist attacks killed around 3,000 Americans in New York City, Washington, D.C., and Pennsylvania. Thousands more were injured. The attacks caused the U.S. government to rethink its approach to national security. The Department of Homeland Security (DHS) was created soon after the attacks. The U.S. Immigration and Naturalization Service had regulated immigration and citizenship matters since 1933. Its functions were absorbed into the DHS. The Border Patrol also became a part of the DHS.

SPOTLIGHT ON

The Border Patrol

The U.S. Border Patrol was established by a congressional act on May 28, 1924. Mounted guards had patrolled the borders with Mexico and Canada since 1904. But they lacked the funding to keep a close eye on the borders at all times. Many illegal immigrants were able to slip past them. The federal government gave closer attention to illegal entry when the Johnson-Reed Act of 1924 established strict quotas. The Border Patrol's activities were expanded after the 9/11 terrorist attacks. The organization was made a branch of the newly formed Department of Homeland Security in 2002. It works to make sure that terrorists and dangerous weapons do not enter the country.

A FIRSTHAND LOOK AT
THE SECURE FENCE ACT OF 2006

The Secure Fence Act's supporters believed that it would prevent entry of illegal immigrants, terrorists, and drugs. But it did not live up to these expectations. See page 60 for a link to view the entire text of the act online.

President George W. Bush approved the Secure Fence Act in 2006. It called for a fence to be constructed along 700 miles (1,100 kilometers) of the U.S.-Mexico border. Cameras and radar would be used along the border. The program proved to be too expensive and less effective than thought. It was put on hold in 2010.

Border fences are not always effective at keeping illegal immigrants out of the country.

Illegal immigrants provide an inexpensive labor force for many American farms.

Border security is only one of the difficult issues raised by immigration in the 21st century. One 2005 study estimates that there are more than 11 million illegal immigrants in the United States. Most of them have come from Mexico and other Latin American countries. This has led to widespread discrimination against people from these countries. Illegal immigrants make up an estimated 5 percent of the country's labor force. Most work seasonal jobs doing farmwork, construction, and food preparation. Many American workers see them as a threat to employment.

Illegal immigration is a highly controversial issue.

Controversy

Illegal immigrants are often willing to work for less pay and longer hours than legal U.S. citizens. American workers complain that this removes the need for employers to improve pay and working conditions. Employers respond that immigrants are often harder workers than legal citizens are.

Some citizens direct their frustration with illegal immigrants toward Mexican American citizens. Politicians must balance these frustrations with the rights of Hispanic citizens. States such as California have large Hispanic populations. The use of the Spanish language in these places continues to be a controversial issue. Some citizens believe that English should be adopted as the national language.

They reason that using more than one language divides the nation. Other people argue that an English-only law would compromise the rights of citizens whose first language is not English.

There are no simple answers to the questions raised by immigration. The United States was founded by immigrants. It was built and developed by immigrants. Yet immigration has always been a controversial issue. People often mistrust those who come from different religious or cultural backgrounds. But cultural differences have made the United States the country it is today. Only time will tell how the nation will deal with immigration in the future.

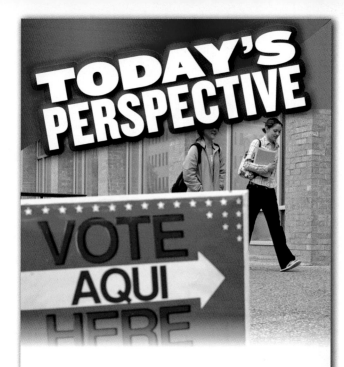

TODAY'S PERSPECTIVE

VOTE AQUI HERE

In 1907, President Theodore Roosevelt wrote, "We have room for but one language in this country, and that is the English language." The idea has stirred broad debate in the century since it was written. The English-only movement has succeeded in winning support in some states. People who speak Spanish are often discriminated against in these areas. Many people have come to associate the language with illegal immigration. But many of the country's Spanish speakers are legal citizens. A national law making English the country's official language has yet to be passed. The country's Spanish-speaking population is growing rapidly. Politicians know that such laws would anger large numbers of voters.

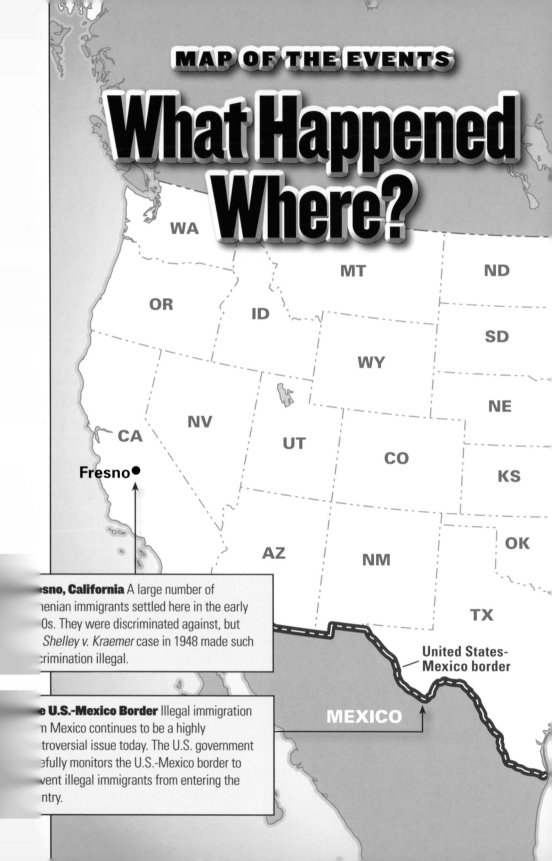

What Happened Where?

WA

MT

ND

OR

ID

SD

WY

NE

NV

CA

UT

CO

KS

Fresno●

AZ

NM

OK

TX

United States-
Mexico border

MEXICO

...esno, California A large number of ...menian immigrants settled here in the early ...0s. They were discriminated against, but ... *Shelley v. Kraemer* case in 1948 made such ...crimination illegal.

...e U.S.-Mexico Border Illegal immigration ...m Mexico continues to be a highly ...troversial issue today. The U.S. government ...efully monitors the U.S.-Mexico border to ...vent illegal immigrants from entering the ...ntry.

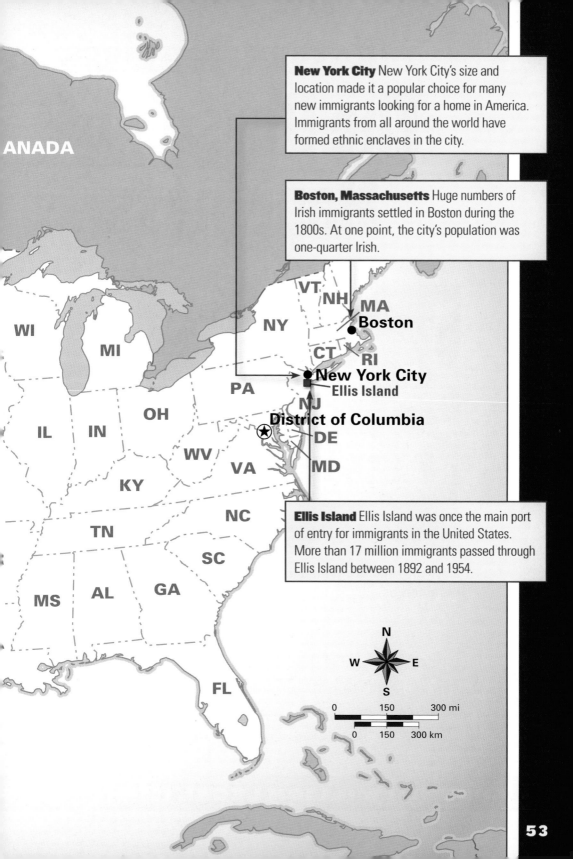

New York City New York City's size and location made it a popular choice for many new immigrants looking for a home in America. Immigrants from all around the world have formed ethnic enclaves in the city.

Boston, Massachusetts Huge numbers of Irish immigrants settled in Boston during the 1800s. At one point, the city's population was one-quarter Irish.

Ellis Island Ellis Island was once the main port of entry for immigrants in the United States. More than 17 million immigrants passed through Ellis Island between 1892 and 1954.

ANADA

WI

MI

VT

NH

MA

Boston

NY

CT

RI

New York City

Ellis Island

PA

NJ

District of Columbia

DE

OH

IL

IN

WV

MD

KY

VA

NC

TN

SC

MS

AL

GA

FL

N
W E
S

0   150   300 mi

0   150   300 km

The Pursuit of Happiness

New citizens are welcomed to the United States with large ceremonies.

Immigration has played a central role in building the United States and defining its culture. It continues to occupy an important place in discussions about economics, education, terrorism, social services, and citizenship. Immigrants have historically been workers, innovators, and businesspeople. They have enriched American life. Each generation's struggles have served to remind American citizens of the liberty they have taken for granted. But their cultural and linguistic differences have given rise to concerns that are all too familiar.

Today's debate over immigration is remarkably similar to the one that led to the Chinese Exclusion Act of 1882. It also resembles the thinly disguised hatreds of the Know-Nothing Party. Although these arguments are similar, we live in a different time. The September 11 attacks showed that the United States was not as secure as its people had believed. The attacks led to stricter immigration rules in an effort to prevent terrorists from entering the country. Such issues of national security will likely continue to influence U.S. immigration law as time goes on.

The September 11 attacks changed the way many Americans think about national security.

COME TO THE UNITED STATES EACH YEAR.

INFLUENTIAL INDIVIDUALS

Paul Revere

Bartholomew Gosnold (1572–1607) was one of the founders of the Jamestown Colony, the first permanent English settlement in America.

John Rolfe (1585–1622) was an influential early member of the Jamestown Colony. He saved the colony from financial ruin by introducing profitable tobacco crops.

Paul Revere (1735–1818) was the son of a French Huguenot immigrant. He joined the militant Sons of Liberty and opposed British colonial oppression. He also alerted the colonial militia of the movement of British troops before the Battles of Lexington and Concord.

Pierre-Charles L'Enfant (1754–1825) was a French immigrant and architect. He fought in the American Revolution and later started an engineering firm in New York City. He designed the street plan of the nation's capital in Washington, D.C.

William Tweed (1823–1878) was the Irish Catholic boss of the Democratic Party in New York City. He created jobs for immigrants who would lend him political support.

Thomas Nast (1840–1902) was a German immigrant who became a well-known political cartoonist for *Harper's Weekly*. He regularly made fun of William Tweed's political corruption.

Theodore Roosevelt

Theodore Roosevelt (1858–1919) was the 26th president of the United States. He had strong opinions about immigration. His belief that English should be the only language used in the United States continues to inspire debate today.

George W. Bush (1946–) was the 43rd president of the United States. He oversaw the formation of the Department of Homeland Security and approved the Secure Fence Act of 2006.

George W. Bush

TIMELINE

1607
The Jamestown Colony is founded in Virginia.

1620
The Plymouth Colony is founded in Massachusetts.

1803
The Passenger Vessels Act is passed.

1886
France gives the Statue of Liberty to the United States.

1892
Ellis Island is opened.

1907
The Gentlemen's Agreement between the United States and Japan is signed.

1927
Sacco and Vanzetti are executed.

1952
The Immigration and Nationality Act of 1952 is passed.

1954
Ellis Island is closed.

1986
The Immigration Reform and Control Act is passed.

1862
The first immigration restriction law is passed.

1882
The Chinese Exclusion Act is passed.

1885
The Contract Labor Law is passed.

1911
The Triangle Shirtwaist factory fire kills 146 people.

1920
Sacco and Vanzetti are arrested.

1924
The Johnson-Reed Act is passed; the U.S. Border Patrol is formed.

1990
The Immigration Act of 1990 is passed.

2002
The Department of Homeland Security is formed.

2006
The Secure Fence Act is passed.

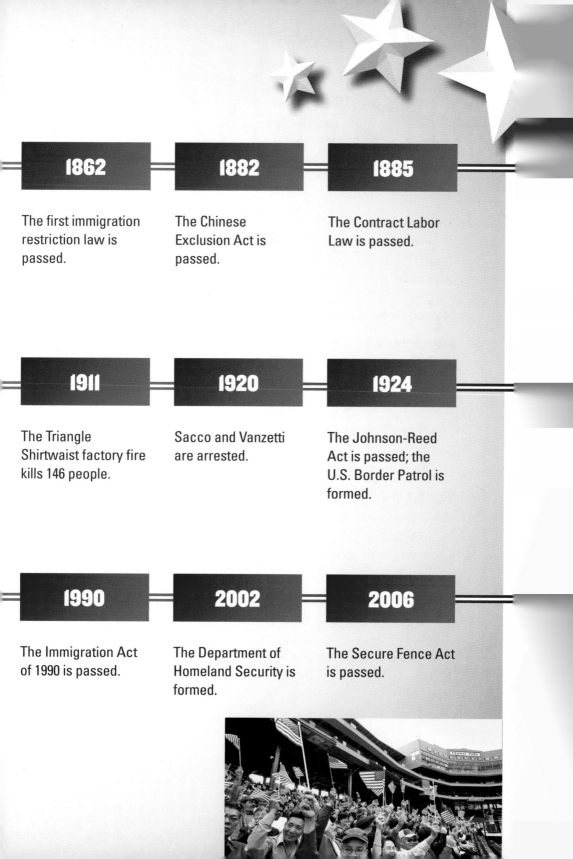

LIVING HISTORY

Primary sources provide firsthand evidence about a topic. Witnesses to a historical event create primary sources. They include autobiographies, newspaper reports of the time, oral histories, photographs, and memoirs. A secondary source analyzes primary sources, and is one step or more removed from the event. Secondary sources include textbooks, encyclopedias, and commentaries.

Ellis Island Ellis Island saw the arrival of more than 17 million immigrants during its years as the country's main port of entry. To watch a video of immigrants arriving in 1903, visit *www.youtube .com/watch?v=8UVl7Lb3N90&feature=related*

The Mayflower Compact The Mayflower Compact helped lay the groundwork for early American governments. To view the text of the compact, visit *http://avalon.law.yale.edu/17th_century/mayflower.asp*

The Secure Fence Act of 2006 The Secure Fence Act of 2006 came about as a result of the United States' concern with national security after the September 11, 2001, terrorist attacks. To read the act online, visit *www.gpo.gov/fdsys/pkg/PLAW-109publ367/pdf/PLAW -109publ367.pdf*

Thomas Nast's Political Cartoons Thomas Nast drew many political cartoons portraying William Tweed as a greedy man who would do whatever it took to become more powerful. See one of Nast's cartoons online by visiting *http://cartoons.osu.edu/nast/images /the_brains100.jpg*

RESOURCES

Books

Brezina, Corona. *America's Political Scandals in the Late 1800s: Boss Tweed and Tammany Hall*. New York: Rosen, 2004.

Haerens, Margaret. *Illegal Immigration*. Chicago: Greenhaven, 2006.

Landau, Elaine. *Ellis Island*. New York: Children's Press, 2008.

Landau, Elaine. *Sacco and Vanzetti*. New York: Children's Press, 2004.

Landau, Elaine. *The Triangle Shirtwaist Factory Fire*. New York: Children's Press, 2005.

Petrini, Catherine M. *The Italian Americans*. San Diego: Lucent, 2002.

Stefoff, Rebecca. *A Century of Immigration: 1820-1924*. New York: Marshall Cavendish Benchmark, 2007.

Web Sites

National Park Service—Ellis Island
www.nps.gov/elis/index.htm
Learn about the history of Ellis Island and find out how you can see it for yourself.

PBS Kids—Big Apple History: Coming to America
http://pbskids.org/bigapplehistory/immigration/index-flash.html
Learn more about New York City's role in immigration through history.

Scholastic—Immigration: Stories of Yesterday and Today
http://teacher.scholastic.com/activities/immigration/index.htm
See what immigration was like for people in 1920, 1933, and today.

Visit this Scholastic Web site for more information on immigration: www.factsfornow.scholastic.com

GLOSSARY

communism (KAHM-yuh-niz-uhm) a way of organizing the economy of a country so that all land, property, businesses, and resources belong to the government or community, and the profits are shared by all

deportation (dee-por-TAY-shuhn) the act of sending someone back to the country from which that person came

discrimination (diss-krim-uh-NAY-shuhn) unfair treatment of others based on age, race, gender, or other factors

economic (e-kuh-NAH-mik) relating to the system of producing, distributing, and consuming goods and services

ethnic enclaves (ETH-nik ON-klayvz) groups of people with common traits and customs who live together in a foreign territory

exploited (ik-SPLOIT-id) treated unfairly for the advantage of others

immigrants (IM-uh-gruhnts) people who move from one country to another and settle there permanently

indentured servants (in-DEN-churd SIR-vuhnts) people who are bound to work for a certain period of time in exchange for food, housing, transport from overseas, and land

legislature (LEJ-iss-lay-chur) the part of government that is responsible for making and changing laws

naturalize (NACH-ur-uh-lize) to give a person who was born in one country citizenship in another

quotas (KWOH-tuhz) fixed amounts of something

refugees (REF-yoo-jeez) people who are forced to leave their homes or countries to escape war, religious persecution, or a natural disaster

rural (ROOR-uhl) of or having to do with the countryside, country life, or farming

urban (UR-buhn) having to do with or living in a city

INDEX

Page numbers in *italics* indicate illustrations.

ABOUT THE AUTHOR

Peter Benoit is a graduate of Skidmore College in Saratoga Springs, New York. His degree is in mathematics. He has been a tutor and educator for many years. Peter has written more than two dozen books for Children's Press. He has written about ecosystems, disasters, and Native Americans, among other topics. He is also the author of more than 2,000 poems.